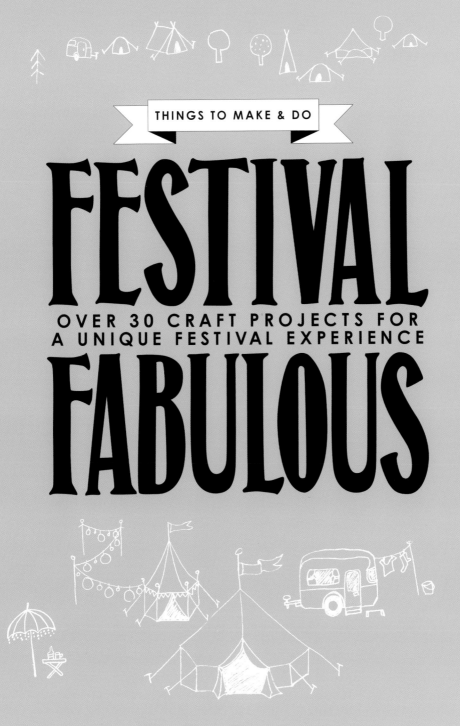

THINGS TO MAKE & DO

FESTIVAL

OVER 30 CRAFT PROJECTS FOR
A UNIQUE FESTIVAL EXPERIENCE

FABULOUS

Ros Badger ❧ Christine Leech

PHOTOGRAPHY BY
JOANNA HENDERSON

FOR OUR BELOVED FAMILIES AND FESTIVAL FRIENDS

Publishing Director Jane O'Shea
Commissioning Editor Lisa Pendreigh
Editorial Assistant Harriet Butt
Pattern Checker Luise Roberts
Creative Director Helen Lewis
Art Director and Designer Christine Leech
Photographer Joanna Henderson
Models May Douglas & Isabel Adomakoh-Young
Production Director Vincent Smith
Production Controller Stephen Lang

First published in 2015 by
Quadrille Publishing Ltd
Pentagon House
52–54 Southwark Street
London SE1 1UN
www.quadrille.co.uk

Quadrille is an imprint of Hardie Grant.
www.hardiegrant.com.au

Quadrille
craft

www.quadrillecraft.com

If you have any comments or queries regarding the
instructions in this book, please contact us at
enquiries@quadrille.co.uk

British Library Cataloguing-in Publication Data
A catalogue record for this book is availble from the
British Library.

ISBN: 978 184949 627 8

Printed in China

Contents

Foreword

Often described these days as the world's muddiest catwalk, festivals are no longer just about getting a ticket and getting there. In the ten years or so since I - along with several others - founded Port Eliot Festival in Cornwall, festival wear, festival chic, in fact anything with fringing or Kate Moss in tow, is now tagged festival style, and has become a focus of summer fashion pages. Festival style cannot be quantified, but the closest you can get to it is to be prepared. It means not having to think too hard about what you are going wear, so you can focus on having a good time. And the fun thing is then adorning yourself, or your tent, or whatever you will, as the weekend progresses. On a festival site something happens, there is a kind of magic that sets in and you forget about the real world, and wearing a floral head dress all day, and night, becomes a possibility, if not an absolute necessity.

Last summer we gave Ros and Christine an area at Port Eliot Festival, which we called The Badger's Sett. We gave them a lawn with a huge lime tree, a yurt, a handful of trestle tables and chairs and they gave us their wonderful imaginations. All weekend they ran cool and crafty workshops. They never sat down. The area was an instant hit - everytime I visited or walked by, I could see very happy people being taught by the Badgers how to make something useful AND beautiful.

In this wonderful book of how to have fun with proper festival style, there are so many amazing ideas for how to make your festival weekend just that little bit better. But my favourite thing Ros and Christine have come up with is their showertime dress. It is GENIUS! I am a sucker for anything towelling anyway, but this dress is just the chicest thing I have seen for a long time. With a simple rope neck, you put it on before you saunter off to the shower block, (which is never exactly a highlight of a festival weekend) and stash your shampoo, hairbrush and clean knickers in its big patch pockets. Now *that* is fabulous festival style.

LADY CATHERINE ST GERMANS
PORT ELIOT, CORNWALL

Introduction

Creativity at festivals is all about taking part in the creation of a unique enchanted world. Fields are lit up with sparkling lights, peppered with human peacocks: a magical, mystical, otherworldly environment only exists for a few short days and then disappears, leaving nature to reclaim her space.

In these microcosms it is totally normal to have glitter on your eyelids while drinking your morning coffee or to sport a homemade silk pompom on your head while hula hooping. Unlike normal environs, ingenuity is expected at festivals and many people go to them precisely because the experience allows their imagination to run wild.

Festival fields are lit up with sparkling lights, peppered with human peacocks.

While writing our programme of workshops for The Badger's Sett at Port Eliot Festival, we had so many ideas to share that the only way to pass on our fabulous crafting secrets was by publishing this book. We have combined our years of design and craft knowledge to create beautiful, useful and individual projects that will make any camping experience unique. We have interrogated friends for their top tips and had various accomplices sneak backstage to discover how the artists glamp it up. Remember, it is always worth the effort to glam up your tent; your tealight-lit porch bedecked with garlands, lanterns and flags should be the one other revellers envy as they stumble past to their drab unlit tent.

HOW TO USE THIS BOOK

This book is filled with projects and ideas to enable you to have the Best Festival Ever. From what to pack and what to eat, to how to make your own bespoke headdresses and tent ornaments. The front section is full of inspirational pictures and ideas and the back is packed with instructions and templates. We are here to show you how to make your camping space and yourself truly shine. All that is left to say is **HAVE A FABULOUS FESTIVAL.**

ROS & CHRISTINE

Festival *noun*

➤ **An organised series of concerts, plays, or films*, typically one held annually in the same place over several days**

SYNONYMS fete, fair, gala day, gala, carnival, fiesta, jamboree, pageant.

EXAMPLES Glastonbury, Coachella, Burning Man, Exit, Tomorrowland, Latitude, Port Eliot.

Festivalgoer *noun*

➤ **One who attends a festival**

IDENTIFIABLE MARKINGS often found with dried mud reaching knee height. Elaborate face paint depicting fairy, flower or disco warrior.

DRESS part sun worshipper, part storm chaser.

FAVOURED POSITION arms aloft - warm cider in one hand - other raised desperately trying to find phone signal**. Flat out - face up or face down depending on time of day/night.

HABITAT hot sweaty tent at maximum capacity, cold damp tent not really big enough for two.

DIET Cider. Strange unidentifiable hot dish from whichever stall has the shortest queue. Gin. Chocolate. Water - not necessarily yours.

*more often all at once **Unless it's day two when all batteries are flat. Everywhere.

COVERED COAT HANGERS

page 73

SCALLOP
CAPE
ᵗᵗ page 99 ᵗᵗ

POLKA DOT KIT BAG
page 62

FESTIVAL
MANDALA
⨯ page 64 ⨯

SAILCLOTH AWNING

page 68

Whether staying in a tent or a camper van finding shelter at a festival will be essential at some point, either from the sun or the rain. Given that you won't always be able to camp under a shady tree, you may have to supply your own. This awning is made from a 40-year-old sail. Reusing fabrics that have had a previous life gives your finished project a ready made history and a story to tell round the camp fire. Yacht sails are huge and three awnings were made from this one, making it an economical project as well as a gorgeous one.

FLOWER & RAFFIA GARLAND
page 72

REFLECTIVE CROWN
page 70

MINI RUCKSACK
page 78

TENT PEG
FLAGS

↠ page 74 ↞

Eat breakfast,
Don't eat breakfast.
Party till 6,
sleep till 4.
Hug a stranger.
Dance.
Watch the stars.

Do what you like
when you like;
you're on
festival time.

BLANKET BUNTING
page 81

POCKET
ORGANISER

⇥ page 82 ⇤

⚡ CAMPING ⚡

Your tent, yurt, caravan, camper or converted ice cream van will be your home away from home at festival time. Arrive early to get the best pitch... Close (but not too close) to the portaloos, near a stand pipe and a landmark. Mark out your territory with bunting (p71, 81, 85) and flags (p74, 77) (but don't expect the boundary necessarily to be respected!) Wooden crates are great for transporting your stuff and double up as bedside tables or seats during the festival, or customise an old trolley to wheel things round (p108). Hangers (p73) and a pocket organiser (p82) will help keep the chaos in order and don't forget the number one camping rule.
No shoes inside the tent.

FESTIVAL
BLANKET

page 88

LACE CROWN
↠ page 92 ↞

BIRDWING PONCHO

page 94

PAINTED FEATHERS
page 91

PLAITED
BASKET

⚜ *page 100* ⚜

Sunglasses

Big, bigger, biggest – Go loud, be proud, they'll be your sunny day accessory or hangover fashion friend.

HATS

Beanies are for cooler nights and bad hair days. Trilbys are for sunshine and showers.

Pockets

Anything with pockets is invaluable at a festival. If you have a favourite top or dress that is pocketless, sew patch pockets on to the front or open a side seam and add one in.

Wellies

Stick to classic colours and a trusted brand - wet socks are No Fun.

ANKLE BOOTS

Flip flops are fine but ankle boots are the ones that are going to protect you from dancing feet, dew covered grass and suspicious mounds of muck.

Shorts

Wet jeans are not nice. Shorts and bare legs or shorts and tights are much better.

Sequins

If ever there was a place where the daytime sequin was acceptable then it's the fields of a festival. Gold, silver, muliticoloured, if you're going to wear them, wear them all.

Vintage

But nothing too precious as there's always a chance it may get lost, ruined or swapped for champagne.

WATERPROOF JACKET

Substantial with a hood.

Headdress

Feathers, flowers and pompoms. Butterflies, beads and baubles. Anything goes on a headdress. Small and delicate or big and bold, you're not truly festival fabulous until you are sporting a signature head piece.

FRIENDSHIP
BRACELETS
⇢ page 104 ⇠

DECORATED TROLLEY
page 108

BAMBOO
CANE
STREAMERS
≫ page 109 ≪

✂ BUNTING ✂

Bunting and garlands, like flags, are a staple at festivals. Use them to decorate the inside of your tent or to define your area when camping with groups of friends. The simplest no-sew bunting can be made from strips of old silk scarves like this one (p85). It's so lightweight it flutters in the slightest of breezes and folds up to nothing. Old blankets make a more traditional bunting (p81), for a change try oblongs or pennant shapes instead of triangles.

BUNNY EARS BOW
⚜ page 111 ⚜

CAMPSITE
LANTERN

✤ page 130 ✤

❧ HEADDRESSES ❧

A festival is not a festival without people parading around in a variety of hair bands, hats and headdresses. Be it a simple band with pompoms attached or an elaborate confection of silk flowers and ribbons, you are not fully embracing the festival spirit if you're not adorned like a Midsummer sprite.

Though most festivals sell garlands and some have workshops to make your own, there's nothing like wearing your own bespoke headdress. Learn how to make your own giant bunny ears (p111), flower garlands (p72, 112) and elegant crowns (p70, 92) or try making pompoms (p66) and feathers (p126) to create your own unique headpiece.

SILK FLOWER HEADDRESS
page 112

SHOWERTIME DRESS
✤ page 116 ✤

PATCHWORK
TENT
page 118

MONOGRAM TENT PENNANT
❊ page 77 ❊

WASH BAG ESSENTIALS

Face wipes

oooowww! Pain killers

Lip balm

SUN CREAM

Eyemask

Dry shampoo

BEROCCA

Ear plugs *ssssshhhh!*

Deodorant

TOOTH BRUSH & TOOTH PASTE

Hand sanitiser

travel sizes are perfect

POMPOM
NECKLACE
page 120

FEATHER GARLAND
page 126

CROCHET
GLASS
HOLDERS
page 124

JAM JAR
CHANDELIER
page 128

FOLD OUT PICNIC HAMPER
page 132

mmmmmmm...

Chocolate

GIN IN A TIN
Fancy rice
posh boil in the bag

ENERGY BARS
healthy ones made of dried fruit

Peanut butter
Popcorn
more fun than crisps

Sardines
Flapjack

CHEWING GUM
when brushing your teeth
is just. Too. Much. Effort

Oranges
vitamin C in its own handy packaging

WELLY TOPPERS
✳ page 87 ✳

You've had the

BEST.
TIME.
EVER.

till next time when it's

WAY BETTER
THAN LAST
YEAR

Polka dot kit bag

This kit bag is perfect for ferrying your sleeping bag to your tent. The large pockets are great for stuffing with all your last minute bits and bobs you almost forget when packing.

2 m calico ✳ Basic sewing kit ✳ Tailors' chalk ✳ Household sponges (the denser the better) ✳
Acrylic paint in 3 colours in different shades ✳ Old plates for paint ✳ Bottle lid or cork approx 4
cm diameter for making polka dots ✳ Neon thread ✳ 2 m x 6 cm striped webbing

Cut one 90 x 60 cm rectangle, one 90 x 30 cm rectangle and one 32 cm diameter cirlce from the calico.

To print the fabric

From the sponges cut three triangles of varying sizes roughly 6, 8 and 11 cm high. Use these to print a pattern on the smaller rectangle of your calico. Squeeze the paints out onto old plates.

Do a couple of test prints on scrap fabric first to work out how much pressure you need to apply, to get a good result. This bag was inspired by a mountain and tree scape, but you can experiment with different shapes and patterns. Start with your palest shade then the work down your rectangle getting darker or brighter. In the example shown, pale orange was used first, then brown and finally bright orange.

On the larger rectangle print yellow polka dots randomly over the fabric. Leave both to dry.

To make the drawstring channel

When dry take the smaller rectangle and fold and press a 1 cm double hem along one long edge. Sew in place with the neon thread.

On the larger rectangle turn and press 1 cm hem and then turn and press a 5 cm channel along the top edge. Unfold the channel and turn 1 cm hem along the short edge at each end of the channel (this will prevent fraying when the webbing is drawn through).

Sew the hem in place at either end of the channel and sew along 4 cm down from the top edge. Feed the webbing through the channel but don't gather it together yet.

To make the pockets

Take the smaller rectangle, fold and press a 1 cm double hem along the top long edge then sew with the neon thread.

Place the smaller rectangle on top of the larger piece with the right side up and with the bottom and sides aligned, sew up each side.

Make four equidistant marks along the rectangles for the pockets. Mark straight lines with tailors' chalk then sew from the bottom to the hemline.

To make the bag

Beginning on one side of the large rectangle take the circular base of the bag and line it up with the bottom edge of the rectangle. Pin right sides together, leaving a 1 cm seam allowance. Pin 3 cm in from the side and insert the webbing between the two pieces of calico (refer to the fourth illustration on page 79).

Continue pinning around the circle until you reach the other side. Remember to pin the other end of the webbing 3 cm in from the other side. When sewing in a circle it's easier to tack and remove the pins before sewing it up under a sewing machine.

Pin the two long edges together until you reach the channel seam. The turned over hem at the channel will give you a natural line to follow.

Neaten up the raw edges with a zigzag or overlocking stitch then turn the bag right side out and press seams with an iron under a damp cloth.

Festival mandala

This is a colourful decoration for any festival or bell tent. Inspired by beautiful dreamcatchers, which are very much part of festival culture, and also influenced by Mandalas, the ritual symbol of the universe found in Hinduism and Buddhism.

Thread a needle with embroidery thread and then over stitch to attach your doily to the wooden ring. Pass the thread through the fabric from back to front, then return it over the hoop from front to back, repeating this action every 1 cm all the way around until the fabric is taut in the ring. Finish off the thread securely.

Cut the raffia or string at different lengths (which you can also plait if you like) and also any other coloured threads. Attach to the lower arc of the hoop by folding the lengths in two, passing the looped end through the hoop and then the two ends back through the loop. Pull tight around the hoop to secure.

To make the gaffer tape feathers, stick two pieces of tape together, sticky side to sticky side. Fold in half vertically and cut into a feather shape. Snip into the feather to make notches and give it an authentic feathery look.

Sew the pompoms onto the ends of same strings by passing a piece of wool through the pompom and tying it to the string tightly, ensuring it is disguised among the wool.

Loop either the raffia or string twice through your shells to secure and add the beads in the same way. Tie a knot below the hole to stop them from slipping.

Use a second embroidered doily for the fabric feathers although patterned fabric would also work well. Cut feather shapes from the fabric (see template shapes on p139 to give you ideas). Fold the feathers through the middle to make them slightly 3D. Attach using a darning needle, by passing the string or raffia through the top of the fabric and then finish by knotting.

There are two ways to attach the real feathers, either by using neon gaffer tape wrapped around the quill and p onto the string, or by wrapping an end of the string around the quill and sticking together with all-purpose glue.

To finish your mandala adjust the lengths by repositioning the loops of string and raffia around the wooden hoop or by trimming some ends to shorten so your decorations hang at different lengths.

Anything goes with this make so be creative and make an individual piece.

you will need

Needle and embroidery thread to match

A vintage doily

Embroidery hoop with an approximately 2 cm wider, diameter than the doily

Raffia

Coloured string

Basic sewing kit

Neon gaffer tape

Small pompoms (see p66)

Shells razor and limpets with their fps knocked off

Beads

Fabric feathers (see p126)

Painted feathers (see p91)

All-purpose glue

Pompoms

Pompoms are a super versatile craft project. They can be made at any size and from so many more materials than just plain old wool. Use wool, tulle and old silk scarves to make pompoms that adorn jackets, headscarves and more.

In this book we've used simple pompoms made from wool for our Pompom Necklace (p120). We've recycled old silk scarves to make adornments for our Silk Flower Headress (p112), and pompom ties for our Scallop Cape (p99). Whether you make them with cardboard or a pompom maker, once you've learned or remembered how to make a pompom there are endless posibilites for how to use them. Ones made from tulle can make brightly coloured headbands or earrings. Hang them in bunches as a decoration, string them together to make a garland or use them individually or grouped together to make colourful festival headbands. If you are making wool ones then how you wind the wool determines the outcome of the pom. Wrap two or three colours of wool together to get a milticoloured speckled effect or wrap in bands of colour for a stripey one. Remember the colour you use first will ultimately be in the middle of your pom pom. Large or small a pompom is a true festival friend.

you will need

Card (old cereal packet or similar) ✳ Ruler
Scissors ✳ Wool, silk scarves or tulle

✤ From the card cut two doughnut shapes. For a medium sized pompom make them with a 10 cm diameter and a 5 cm hole. Place one on top of the other and cut a slit in both.

✤ Wrap the wool evenly around both doughnuts feeding it through the hole each time (the slit will make this process easier), until the inner hole is completely full.

✤ Use sharp scissors to snip through all the wool around the edge until you can see the cardboard inside.

✤ Separate the two rings slightly then take another piece of wool and wrap it securely around the middle of your pompom between the two pieces of card.

✤ Pull as tight as you can and knot. Leave a long length on this piece so you can easily tie your pompom to other things.

✤ Remove the cardboard rings and fluff out the pompom. Trim any straggly bits of wool.

➻ To make a fabric or silk scarf pompom, use 1-2 cm wide strips then follow the instructions above. When one strip finishes wrap another over the top and continue.

Sailcloth awning

Create your own unique shelter using an
old sail to keep you cool and dry.

Old sail (alternatively you could use any large canvas fabric, preferably water repellent)
Scissors ✳ Sewing machine and strong thread ✳ 50 cm wide webbing or strong tape (if you are not using the sail's rigging) ✳ 3 D-rings, 4 cm size (optional ✳ 10–12 m of 10 mm rope or yachting rope (reflective cord is available)
2 m wooden pole with a 6 cm x 8 mm diameter screw-in metal dowel
screwed 3 cm vertically into the top end

- Your finished awning will be in the shape of an isosceles triangle with the two angled sides of an equal length of 285 cm and a base length of 270 cm (straight vertical from base to top 290 cm).

- Begin by laying out your sail and see if it offers any areas that can be built into your design. Here the sail's orginal 99 was used in the finished awning and the guy ropes were attached to the existing large eyelets at the bottom edge. If you don't have these then use 3 x 4 cm D-rings (see instructions below).

- In some instances you may be required to remove an oversized eyelet from the head of the sail. This is traditionally used to attach the sail to the the mast head. You will need to re-stitch it back onto the top point of your awning as an opening for the wooden pole or third guy rope, if your sail doesn't have this then add a D ring here too.

- Because the sail is so large there will be certain areas of it that will look better than others. You will need to cut out the best bits to sew together, in order to form the isosceles traingle of the awning. Once you have cut out your parts, sew them together using a zgzag stitch on a sewing machine, like a patchwork to make the triangle shape. However if you prefer a simpler life then cut out the triangle shape from your fabric in the first instance. If you don't think your machine is tough enough to handle the sailcloth, you could use a tough fabric glue instead or a staple gun.

- If you are adding D-rings then do so as follows. Cut out 3 x 15 cm pieces of webbing or tape. Fold each in half through the straight edge of the D-ring then stitch one to each corner of the awning, reinforcing it with an extra piece of fabric between the webbing and the sailcloth.

To hang the awning

- Option 1: Divide your rope into three and add one piece to each corner either through the D-ring or eyelet hole using an overhand or reef knot to secure. Use these ropes to attach the awning to three solid points to create shade, i.e. two could be attached to your camper van or tent and one to a tree or a second tent or van.

- Option 2: (shown in the photograph) Divide your rope into three and add one piece to each of the two bottom corners, either through the D-ring or eyelet hole using an overhand or reef knot to secure. Use these ropes to attach to two points on either your camper van or tent.

- Finally thread the third rope through the eyelet or D-ring then add the metal dowel at the top of the 2 m pole. Manoeuvre the pole into place to hold the awning taut, and use the rope like a tent guy rope, attaching it to a tent peg in the ground.

Reflective crown & bunting

While at Port Eliot festival we were inspired by the brilliant reflective triangular bunting that Juliet Roberts made, enabling her to find her tent at night. We have taken this idea one step further by creating a crown that glows when caught in a direct beam of a light so your friends will never lose you.

THE CROWN

you will need

15 cm square of reflective fabric
All-purpose glue ✻ Cardboard ✻ Basic sewing kit
53 cm of 10 mm coloured elastic

To begin fold the fabric in half, wrong sides together and stick with an all-purpose glue.

When completely dry, make a cardboard template for an isosceles triangle, 7 cm for the the long sides and a 5 cm base. Cut out five of these from the fabric.

Pin the first triangle onto one side of the elastic in the centre, 5 mm up from the bottom edge (if you are using 10 mm wide elastic). Space the others equally on each side, about 1 cm apart, leaving the last 12 cm elastic at each end free.

Stitch into place, ideally with a sewing machine – if you do it by hand use a back stitch to secure. You may have to slightly stretch the elastic as you sew.

Finally overlap the two ends of elastic by 1 cm and stitch firmly together to finish your crown.

This crown also looks great made from faux leather in gold or neon colours.

THE BUNTING

you will need

50 x 90 cm of reflective fabric ✻ Cardboard
Basic sewing kit ✻ 5 m of nylon piping cord, similar to tent guy ropes ✻ All-purpose glue

Make a template from card by firstly drawing a diamond shape with all the sides measuring 10 cm and with a horizontal axis of 12 cm, although you can adjust to make any size you like.

Cut out 30 diamonds.

Fold the diamonds in half, wrong sides together to make double sided triangles, then place the cord into the fold and stick the reflective fabric together using an all-purpose glue. Continue adding all the triangular flags along the cord spacing each one about 10 cm apart and leaving the first and last 5 cm of cord free.

Only gluing up to 5 mm from the fold will allow you to slide the triangles along the cord. If you prefer them to be secure just continue to glue up to the fold.

Flower & raffia garland

you will need

Plastic blossom type flower stem or small plastic flowers on a long stem

Florists' wire or fuse wire

A selection of different coloured raffia to match or contrast with your flowers

Scissors

Silk pompoms (see p66)

Simple to make, this impressive headdress can be embellished in a multitude of ways. Try adding mini pompoms, shells or feathers for a unique piece.

Bend the stem of the plastic blossom into a circle to form a crown shape that will fit around your head. Twist together to hold the shape. Next, wind a bit of florist's wire or fuse wire around the join to secure.

Attach different lengths of raffia on one side of the garland. To do this fold the raffia in half, wrap the folded end around the plastic stem, passing the two loose ends through the loop and pulling it tight.

Continue adding raffia until you have enough strands in different colours and lengths to look good.

Add a silk pompom (p66) to the plastic stem by tying it tightly in place, using the long ends of the pompom centre.

To finish

Experiment by plaiting some of the raffia and tie a knot at the end to stop it unravelling.

Add one or two flowers (easily removed from the plastic stem) by threading the raffia through the centre of each flower and tying a double knot to stop it falling off.

Covered coat hangers

Lots of strips of shredded fabric approximately 5 mm wide by a minimum of 50 cm

Scissors

Wire coat hangers.

All-purpose glue

Coat hangers are a festival necessity and covered ones will not only protect your precious festival fabrics from damp floors and the lack of an iron but stop your clothes from slipping off too. They also have a number of other uses, doubling up as a hook for bunting or fairy lights.

❦ Begin by shredding lots of strips of fabric. Use a variety of different fabric weights for your hangers, from linen and ticking to an old silk scarf that has seen better days.

❦ To make the ribbons, make a series of snips. 5 mm apart into the fabric along the shortest edge, then rip down to the end.

❦ To wrap the hanger begin at the hook. Put a blob of glue on the end of the ribbon and start wrapping it tightly all around the wire overlapping as you go. NB the glue will dry hard and clear so don't worry if it looks milky at first.

❦ When you get towards the end of the first ribbon, tie it back on itself in a knot around the hanger. Add another blob of glue then start wrapping with the second piece of shredded fabric, covering the knot from the end of the last piece.

❦ Continue until the hanger is covered. Secure the end with glue, trim and leave to dry.

Tent peg flags

This hotch potch of flags will flutter prettily around your tent and also warn people of the impending danger of the dreaded tent peg.

Several different linen fabrics, plain and patterned at least 27 cm square ✶ Scissors ✶ Iron
Thread to match the fabrics ✶ Basic sewing kit ✶ Bondaweb ✶ Thin muslin ✶ Staple gun
✶ Short bamboo canes or wooden dowel approx 40 cm long ✶ Ribbons

To make the flags

The basis of these flags is a simple 25 cm square. These can either be made from one piece of fabric or several sewn together, for a patchwork effect. The most straightforward flag to make is a square of fabric with frayed edges. To fray the edges, simply pull away the loose threads at the edge of the fabric until you get about 1 cm of fringing. If you do this to one side before you cut the rest of the square you will have a perfectly straight edge to use as a guide for the rest of the square.

Alternatively you could hem the flag with a 0.5 cm double turned hem on all sides. If you are hemming the flag start with a 27 cm square of fabric.

The patchwork flags are sewn together using a flat fell seam. This means you will have no unsightly raw edges on either side of the flag.

To make a frayed edge two tone flag

❧ Choose two pieces of fabric and cut each into a 25 x 14 cm rectangle. Take one piece of fabric and iron a 10 mm hem along one long side.

❧ Place the other piece of fabric on top of the first so it sits inside the hem flap. Pin the two pieces together and stitch along the folded hem.

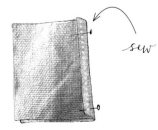

sew

❧ Unpin and open the second piece of fabric back over the seam (like turning the pages of a book). Press flat with an iron.

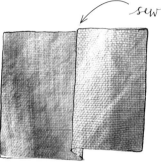

sew

❧ Run another line of stitches parallel to the first just catching the first piece of fabric. Press again. Fray the outer edges. You could also hem around these flags but remember to allow for a 5 mm seam allowance when cutting.

❧ Use this method to create several different patterned flags.

To make the appliqué motifs

❧ Copy the template of the bird from p140. Trace the individual parts onto the smooth side of a piece of Bondaweb. Roughly cut it out.

❧ Place the Bondaweb shapes onto the wrong side of your chosen coloured fabrics and use an iron (with no steam) to fix the Bondaweb in place. ⟫→

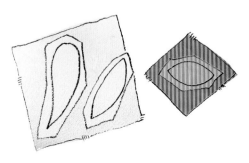

🌿 Carefully cut out each of the pieces and peel away from the Bondaweb's protective paper.

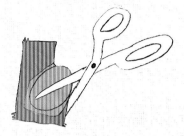

To make the appliqué birds and flowers.
🌿 Onto a thin piece of fabric (muslin or sheeting) trace the outline of the bird. Like a jigsaw place the different pieces of fabric inside the outline building up the shape of the bird (some pieces will overlap). Cover with a damp cloth and press with an iron.

🌿 Finish off your appliqué with a freehand machine embroidery stitch all around the edge of the bird. Many sewing machines come with a special foot for this type of embroidery or you can buy them separately. Follow your machine instructions for attaching the foot and how to embroider.

🌿 Machine stitch around the bird. You can create a nice doodle effect by not removing the bird from the machine until every part of the bird is outlined, this will mean some lines are repeated more than once.

🌿 The heart and flower patch is made in the same way.

🌿 Use a staple gun or small nails to fix the flags to the bamboo canes. Decorate with ribbons.

🌿 Trim away the excess thin fabric and place on your chosen flag. Pin in place the bird.

Monogram tent pennant

This monogrammed flag is the perfect way to help your friends track you down in a sea of identical tents.

you will need

Several different fabrics for appliqué motifs

Basic sewing kit

Bondaweb

1 m x 30 cm calico

Ribbon or cord (length will depend on the length of the name)

1 m x 30 cm patterned cotton

2 large metal eyelets and punch (optional)

- Make two appliqué birds and three applique flowers as per the instructions on pages 75–76.

- On the reverse of the calico make a mark in the middle of the fabric 20 cm in from one end. Draw two diagonal lines from this mark to the corners of the fabric. This creates the 'V' of the pennant.

- Pin the birds and flowers in position and freehand machine embroider them in place. Alternatively, you can always Bondaweb the back of the patches and iron on.

- With a air erasable pen write the name or initials of the tents residents between the two birds in joined up script.

- Lay the ribbon or cord on the fabric following this line of your script and, using small stitches, hand sew in place.

- Place the calico right sides together to the patterned cotton and pin. Starting at the flag pole end machine sew the fabric together. Remember to follow the line of the V at the other end. Leave a turning hole.

- Cut away the excess fabric at the 'V' and notch the ends and inner point to allow the fabric to stretch when turned right side out. Turn right side out, sew up the turn hole and press.

- Make two large button holes or insert two large eyelets to attach the flag to the pole.

Mini rucksack

This little rucksack is made from neoprene which means it is light weight and waterproof. Two reasons why it makes this the perfect festival accessory.

you will need

50 x 95 cm of lilac neoprene ✳ Basic sewing kit ✳ Neon thread ✳ 7 metal eyelets 2 cm diameter
Eyelet punch ✳ 1 large popper ✳ 1 large wooden button ✳ Garden twine in three colours each
2 m in length ✳ Small samples of neoprene in various colours ✳ Small scraps of neoprene
or fabric in different colours ✳ Small paintbrush ✳ Copydex glue

From the neoprene cut a 58 x 21 cm long rectangle. Using the template on p138 cut one base and two flaps. Machine sew the two flaps together right sides out. Leave a 0.5 cm seam allowance at the edge.

To make the straps

Cut a 180 x 7 cm strip from the neoprene; you can make this up from more than one piece if necessary. Fold the two raw edges into the centre so one side overlaps the other reducing the strap's width to about 3 cm. Pin in place then machine sew down the centre of the strap, to hold the fabric in place.

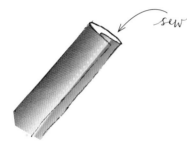

sew

To insert the eyelets

Find the centre point on one long edge of the large rectangle. Make a mark then measure and mark three equidistant points either side of this point. Following the instructions on the eyelet punch, insert the eyelets about 2 cm from the top. If you don't have any eyelets you can reinforce the holes with a machine or hand sew your button holes.

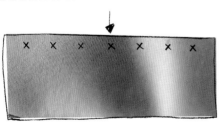

To make the bag

Bring the two short ends of the rectangle around to meet one another, with right side inside, and pin or tack together at the top. Insert the strap ends through the first and last eyelets on either side of the join, with the long ends inside.

Starting at point A on the rucksack base, begin pinning the long rectangle to the base right sides together. When you are 5 cm past point **A** insert one end of the strap. Leave about 1 cm of strap showing. Continue around the base until you are 5 cm from the other side. Insert the other end of the strap. Then pin the short straight edges of the rectangle together.

Tip Lay the strap out flat to make sure it's not twisted. If it is, remove one end of the strap, turn it over and re-insert. ⫸⟶

As you are sewing in a round it helps to tack the fabrics together and remove the pins before sewing. Machine stitch all seams together then turn right side out. Pin then sew the strap to the bag between the first and last eyelets.

To add the flap

Lay the rucksack front side down on a flat surface. Place the flap on the back 7 cm from the top centred over the seam. Pin then sew in place. The straps should sit comfortably either side of the flap.

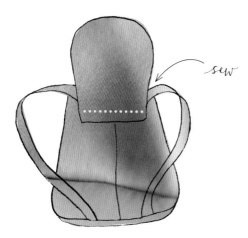

sew

On the inside of the flap, sew one side of the popper at point **B** on the template. Fold the flap down onto the body of the rucksack and mark where the other part of the popper should go. Sew in place. To cover up the stitches left on the outside of the flap, sew the button on top.

To make the drawstring

Following the instructions on p105 make a fishtail plait from the twine. Knot and trim each end then, starting at the central eyelet at the front, weave the drawstring through each one. The drawstring should enter and exit the same eyelet. Knot or bow your drawstring to keep the bag closed when necessary.

To make the decoration

Cut 14 small triangles approximately 25 mm wide and five small rectangles 10 x 5 mm in the neoprene samples. If you don't have samples, felt or any non fraying fabrics would work well.

Alternatively you could paint or stamp on a decoration using acrylic paint (see p63 for a how to).

Following the glue instructions paint a thin layer of glue over one side of each triangle and rectangle, then place on the front of the rucksack building up a pattern. Leave to dry.

Blanket bunting

you will need

Basic sewing kit

Cardboard

Gaffer tape (optional)

Pieces of old blanket and/ or tartan fabrics

Pinking shears

A length of 6 mm twine or piping cord approx 10 m

Sewing machine with piping foot and thread

Bunting, like flags, is a festival staple. This gorgeous bunting is made from upcycled woollen blankets and other small pieces of checkered woolly fabrics. Old moth eaten blankets or fabric scraps would be perfect for this.

- Copy the template from p138 onto card. If you plan on making lots of bunting, cover the edges of your template with gaffer tape to give it a long life.
- Use pinking shears to cut out 40 triangles from your chosen fabrics. When you have enough, fold over 2 cm at the top edge of each (to create a channel for your cord), iron to fix, then lay them on top of each other, in the order you wish them to hang.
- Using the piping foot on your sewing machine, place the cord inside the channel of the first triangle and stitch along the edge, reversing 1 cm at each end to stop any unravelling and to secure your stitching.
- Continue like this until all the triangles are attached to the cord. Snip between each triangle being careful not to cut the cord and spread evenly along the cord. Make a loop at each end of your cord by tying a knot and use this for hanging from trees, your tent, or anywhere!

→ You can use any fabrics and any size of triangle for this bunting, or alternatively you could cut out oblongs and work to make bunting using the same method.

Pocket organiser

This piece of kit will prove essential whether you are in a tent or camper van. It has a variety of pockets to keep anything in it, from your toiletries and hair brush to spare keys, camera, and the odd drink bottle too.

you will need

1 trouser style coat hanger

Up to 5 different ticking fabrics

2 buttons

60 cm of 15 mm wide braid

WS = wrong side
RS = Right side

This pattern can be easily adapted to make a shorter piece with less pockets. You could also add flaps or Velcro to keep the pockets closed and make bespoke sized pockets to fit inside your campervan cupboards.

- Measure the crossbar of your coat hanger, add 4 cm to this width then cut your largest piece of fabric to make the background. This one measured 40 cm by 112 cm long. (This allows for a 2 cm seam allowance on each side with 6 cm at the top and 2 cm along the bottom edge).

- Cut four pockets, **A, B, C, D**; the dimensions are for a 36 cm width hanger so adjust accordingly if your hanger is wider or narrower. **A** being the bottom pocket.

  A: 30 x 78 cm (vertical stripes)
  B: 25 x 60 cm (vertical stripes)
  C: 20 x 64 cm (horizontal stripes)
  D: 18 x 66 cm (horizontal stripes)
  NB the width measurements here allows for the pocket pleats.

- Cut three pieces of braid, two at 16 cm and one at 23 cm.

- An iron is essential when making this as it helps keep the work neat and even, while saving on time too.

- Begin by pressing over the side edges to the WS on both the long edges of the main piece, first by 0.5 cm then again by 1.5 cm. Stitch down each side approximately 0.75 cm in from the inner folded edge.

- Work on all four pockets as follows: At the top edge, fold over by 0.5 cm (WS together) press, then by 1.5 cm and press. Fold over both sides by 0.5 cm and press. Stitch the top hem only. Then fold over the sides again by 1.5 cm this time and press. ⟫⟶

On pockets **B**, **C** & **D** only, fold over the bottom edge, WS together, by 2 cm and press to create the bottom hem edge.

On pocket **C** only attach, the loop used for hanging keys and tea towels, among other things, fold in half the 23 cm braid. Fold the cut ends 2 cm over the top edge of the pocket, 29 cm from the right-hand side (RS facing) and stitch in place to secure.

Attach pocket A

Place the pocket with WS to the RS of the main piece, matching the bottom edges. *Find the centre of both pieces and secure them together at this point with a pin. Open the 1.5 cm section of one side hem on the pocket and fold it over to the WS of the main piece to enclose the edge. Repeat on the other side. Stitch down both sides of the pocket from top to bottom, 0.75 cm in from the edge.**

Divide the width of pocket **A** into three 26-cm sections and mark the divisions with two pins. Mark two points, 8 cm in from both outside edges on the back piece. Match a pin on the pocket to each mark then pin the pocket to the back at this point. Stitch down from the top edge of the pocket to the bottom edge. Using the iron press, creating three shoe type pockets. Pin so that the work is flat. Then fold over the bottom edges by 0.5 cm to the wrong side and press in place. Press again to make a 2 cm hem to the WS and stitch in place across the width, hemming and securing the bottom of the pocket at the same time.

Attach pocket B

Line up the bottom edge of pocket **B** horizontally onto the back piece, 5 cm above the top of pocket **A**. Follow the instructions for pocket **A** from * to **. Stitch a seam down the centre of the work from the top to bottom of pocket **B**. Then press a vertical fold 10 cm in from either side, match this to the outside edges and press again to form the two side pleats. Pin in place and stitch straight across the 36 cm bottom edge to secure the two pockets and hem. NB inverted pleats are on the outside edge only of both pockets.

Attach pocket C

Line up the bottom edge of pocket **C** horizontally onto the back piece, 1.5 cm above pocket **B**. Follow the instructions for pocket **A** from * to **.

Mark the back piece, 11 cm in from the RS (facing) then match this to 24 cm in from the pocket edge. Stitch a vertical seam from the top of **C** to the bottom attaching it to the back. Stitch a second vertical seam 7 cm towards the centre of both pocket and back. Make a third seam, 6 cm further over towards the left of the background but 14 cm over on the pocket.

Iron the three pockets flat creating the inverted pleated sides and a fourth completely flat pocket. Stitch across the 36 cm bottom edge of **C** attaching it to the back piece.

Attach pocket D

Line up the bottom edge of pocket **D** horizontally onto the back piece, 3 cm above pocket **C**. Follow the instructions for pocket **A** from * to **. Match the centre of **D** to the centre of the back piece and stitch vertically in place.

Iron the two pockets flat creating inverted pleated sides on either side of each pocket and stitch across the 36 cm bottom edge of **D**.

Fold the two 16 cm pieces of braid in half, fold over the the ends by 2 cm and stitch this loop onto the back piece only half way between each pocket. Sew the buttons to the pocket and use the folded braid as a loop.

Finally fold the top of your work over by 0.5 cm and press, then fold this over the hanger by 6 cm and stitch across as close to the wooden edge as possible. Make a second row of stitching approx 1cm from the first to secure.

Press, hang and use.

SILK SCARF BUNTING

you will need

A selection of coordinated coloured old silk scarves and/or remnants of chiffon fabrics
Scissors ✳ 6 m cord or twine

This a simple no-sew bunting using scarves that have seen better days and other fabric scraps.

🌲🌲 Make a series of cuts along one side of your scarf or fabric 3 cm in to the edge and approximately 2–3 cm apart.

🌲🌲 Tear the fabric to make ribbons, this technique follows the warp of your fabric, creating even widths of frayed strips. Make a number of these at various lengths.

🌲🌲 When you have enough strips group them together, between 2–4 ribbons per bunch is best.

🌲🌲 Attach to the cord. There are two ways to do this, either tie the ribbons on with a tight knot, or fold them in half and place the folded end over the cord and pass the two loose ends back through the loop and pull tight.

🌲🌲 When you have attached all your ribbons to the cord, space them out evenly by sliding them up or down.

Welly toppers

These cool wellington toppers are extremely practical and will keep on keeping on, no matter how many pairs of socks you go through.

you will need

A pair of 4.5 mm (UK 7) knitting needles.

Yarn: 70 g Rowan creative Focus Deep Rose MC plus tiny amount of charcoal grey for cast on edge (optional)

Tapestry needle

Note, this pattern will also work with most Aran weight yarns.

Tension K2, p2 rib, unstretched, 20 sts x 24 rows = 10cm

K2R = Knit into the front of the second stitch on the left needle, then into the first stitch, drop both stitches together.

The finished welly toppers look like cropped leg warmers. The twisted rib is simple to achieve with no need for a cable needle because there is no shaping involved. Adapt the pattern to make matching wrist warmers.

Make 2

- With Grey, cast on 64 sts (if you don't want a contrast edge cast on in your MC).

- Change to MC.

- Rows 1 and 2: *K2, p2* repeat from * to * to end.

- Row 3: *K2R, p2* repeat from * to * to end.

- Row 4: *K2, p2* repeat from * to * to end.

- Repeat these 4 rows 6 times more (28 rows in all).

- Purl the next row.

- Continue in k2 p2 rib only for 34 rows more.

- Cast off in pattern.

- Sew back seam then sew in any loose ends.

- To wear, with the rib facing inwards, pull on over your socks and up to your knees, put on your wellingtons and fold the rib over the top.

⟶ To make wrist warmers cast on 36 sts instead of 56 sts and work 16 cm in twisted rib pattern, cast off. Sew back seam together leaving a 5.5 cm gap for your thumb.

Festival blanket

A blanket is a festival staple. Great to sit on while watching the performers and wrapped round your shoulders, it'll keep you warm as the dusk falls.

you will need

Vintage blanket with a whipstitched edge

A variety of embroidery threads (silks, wool, gold or silver lurex thread are just some examples)

Tapestry needle

Tailors' chalk

Tracing paper

Iron-on transfer pen

Iron-on letters, can be easily found

Inspired by traditional quilts, you can easily make this festival essential using an old woollen blanket. Simply embroider a number of festival names in different colours, threads and stitch styles, to create a unique and a personal heirloom in the process.

- This is a great project to use up an old forgotten blanket. Cut out a piece approximately 140 x 110 cm. NB This could be bigger or smaller depending on how many names you want to include.

- Use a combination of stitch styles and threads to give your blanket added personality and texture by adding iron-on embroidered letters for some of your festival names. This is also a good alternative if you are not a confident sewer.

- Chain stitch, backstitch and threaded running stitch are easy to do and good stitches to use on your blanket, working well on wool. Work in an eclectic mix of styles and colours. NB Refer to page 90 for stitches.

- To freehand embroider your festival names of choice, start draw a baseline of the name onto your blanket using tailor's chalk. Then work basic block letters along your line. Alternatively create a template for each name to trace from.

- To do this, write the festival name you want to feature on your blanket in the font and size of your choice. Trace over the back of your name then, using a specialist iron-on transfer pen. Follow the iron-on transfer instructions that come with your pen.

- Once you have added all the names you wish to include on your blanket, fold over a 1 cm hem and steam iron in place around all the sides. Work a blanket stitch around the edge. If you kept the original blanket stitch on any of the sides when you initially cut out your piece, then work on the remaining sides without any stitching.

SIMPLE EMBROIDERY STITCHES

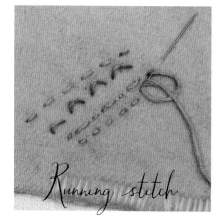

Running stitch

Back stitch

- The simplest of stitches. Starting with your needle at the wrong side of the fabric bring it through to the front then into the back approx 5 mm away. Repeat following the line of your design.

- Varying the lengths of your running stitches can create different effects.

- From the reverse of your fabric bring the needle out at **A**.

- Put your needle in at **B**, then bring it out at **C**.

- Put it back in at **A** and repeat along the line of the word.

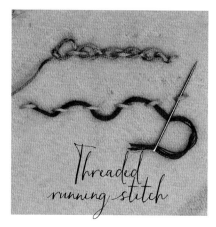

Threaded running stitch

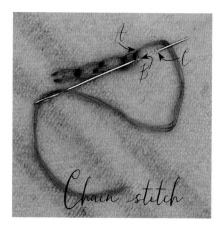

Chain stitch

- You can make a variety of different stitches by threading a second thread through a line of running or back stitch. This second thread doesn't need to go though the fabric at any point, just weave though the stitches.

- Bring your needle through the fabric from the rear at **A**.

- Return the needle into the fabric slightly to the side at **B** and bring it up at **C** without pulling it through.

- Loop the thread around your needle tip and pull through. Insert back into the fabric next to **C**. Repeat.

PAINTED FEATHERS

Painting plain feathers turns them into
ones worthy of any Bird of Paradise

you will need

A selection of feathers real or fake
Acrylic paints ✳ Small soft paintbrushes

Collect a selection of feathers,
the paler the better so aim for
Puddleduck rather than Pigeon.

Thin the paints slightly with water.
Begin painting by brushing diagonally
down the feather following the grain
from the shaft to the feather tip.

Don't worry about being too neat
as the paint colours look nice when
they blend together.

When dry use the other end of your
paintbrush dipped in gold or silver
paint to decorate further.

Use the feathers to decorate hats,
headdresses or make into earrings.

Lace crowns

If ever there was a time to channel Titania Queen of the Fairies then a festival is that time. These crowns are made from lace borders and can be as simple or elaborate as you like.

you will need

Per Crown: 60 cm white lace border the more ornate the better ✻ Basic sewing kit ✻ Piece of plastic
Old tin can or jam jar ✻ All-purpose glue ✻ Old paintbrush ✻ Spray paints in various colours
Small pieces of felt in white, pink, yellow and green approx 10 x 15 cm in size

- Wrap the piece of lace around your head to find the correct size. Overlap where the ends meet by about 2 cm and mark with a pin. Trim the excess lace away.

- Place the lace on a piece of plastic, (a bin bag will do). This is to stop the lace sticking to your work surface when covering it in glue.

- Into an old tin can or jam jar pour 3 cm of glue. Thin the glue by adding a couple of tablespoons of water. Paint this onto the lace with an old paintbrush, working the glue into the lace design using a circular motion. Make sure you cover the lace completely. Flip over and repeat. Allow to dry overnight.

- When dry you will find the lace is much stiffer and will stand up nice and straight. If not, repeat the process above and use a little less water.

To colour the crowns
Place the lace on some old newspaper outside, or in a well ventilated space. Using spray paint completely cover the lace.
It's best to use several thin coats to build up the colour. Allow this to dry for a few minutes then flip over and do the same on the reverse. Leave to dry.

- When completely dry join the two ends of the crown with several stitches in a similar coloured thread to create a circle.

To make the flowers
- Take a piece of pink felt 1.5 x 10 cm and concertina into five layers. Hold at the bottom and trim the top into a curve. Open the strip out and you will have a scolloped edge. Trim to tidy.

- Using a running stitch, sew along the long straight edge of the strip then pull to gather the felt up to create a flower shape.

- Cut a small rectangle of contrasting felt, fold in half and sew into the centre of the flower.

- Make four or five more flowers in various colours and then stitch at intervals around the edge of the crown.

- Smaller flowers can be made by cutting circles of felt in different sizes using scissors or pinking shears. Sew two together and decorate with sequins and beads for added sparkle.

To make the leaves
- Take pieces of green felt 1 x 60 mm and fold in half. Use pinking shears or scissors to cut a leaf shape throughout two pieces of felt, making sure you leave the felt joined up on the fold.

- Open the leaves out and tidy up if necessary. Tie these leaves in a knot and sew onto the crown.

Birdwing poncho

This poncho folds up to nothing, looks fabulous *and* keeps you dry. What's not to like!

you will need

180 cm square nylon/polyester shower curtain ✳ Basic sewing kit ✳ Tailors' chalk pencil ✳ 1 m string
Pinking shears ✳ 1 x 1.4 m pink and white nylon fabric ✳ 50 cm x 1.4 m yellow and purple nylon fabric

To make the poncho

1, Cut the eyelet strip and bottom hem off the shower curtain. Trim the other sides to make a square (approximately 170 cm). Fold in half diagonally and find the centre point. Then fold in half again. Pin all layers of the curtain fabric together.

3, Measure from your neck to between your legs and mark that measurement on the vertical fold of the fabric (**B**). Draw another arc from **B** to intersect the first one.

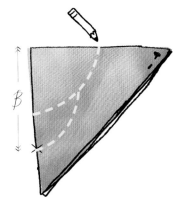

2, Measure from the centre of your neck to your wrist and mark that measurement (**A**) on the fabric. Tie the pencil to a piece of string that is the length of measurement **A**. Tape the end of the string at the fold of the fabric pull the string taut and draw a quarter circle.

4, Using pinking shears cut away the excess fabric and open it out. This is the basic shape of the poncho. Press the long the fold with a cool iron to make the shoulder line. Pin the front and back together on the shoulder line and also further down, this helps stop the poncho slipping around so much as the fabric can be quite tricksy! »—›

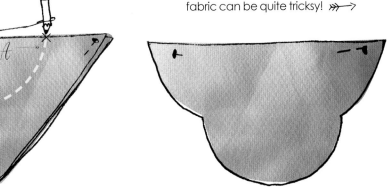

To make the head opening

5, On the front of the poncho find the centre point **C** on the shoulder line. Measure 12 cm to the left and right from this point (**D** and **E**). Measure 6 cm down from point **C** and mark (**F**) then measure another 20 cm down and mark (**G**).

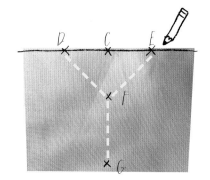

6, Cut a straight line from point **C** to point **G** then diagonally from point **F** up to points **D** and **E**. Finally cut away the fabric between points **D** and **E**. Fold and press a 5 mm hem on both sides of the slash, between points **F** and **G**, then sew.

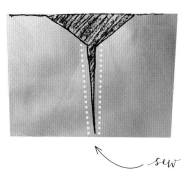

sew

To make the hood

7, You should have enough fabric left over to make the hood. Place two pieces of fabric on top of each other and pin together. Measure and mark a 25 x 40 cm rectangle. On one of the long edges measure 1 cm up from the base and draw a curve. Cut out.

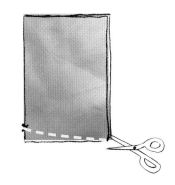

8, If your shower curtain starts to fray use an overlocking stitch. Open out and iron a 5 mm double hem along the longest edge then sew. Fold the hood in half, right sides together then sew up the back seam.

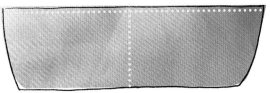

sew

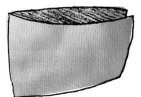

To insert the hood

9. Make sure the hood is the right side out. Starting on the left hand side of the neckline (at the top of the V) pin the hood around the opening, right side together, then tack in place. Sew using an overlocking or zigzag stitch to prevent fraying.

To make the coloured wings

11. To get the best use of your fabrics plan your wing positions carefully. Beginning with the pink wing. Trim the template down cutting away the 'grey' wing section.

12. To make the back wing, draw a right wing, flip the template and draw a left wing (making sure the tops meet). Rotate the template to fit in the space remaining.

To make the wings

10. Enlarge the template on page 139 by approximately 400%, or until the straight edge to the start of the scallop measures the same as **A**. Place the template on the back of the poncho so one straight edge is against one side of the shoulders. Use tailors chalk to draw around the wing scallops. Flip and repeat on the other shoulder. Use pinking shears to cut out the scallops through all layers.

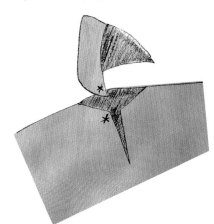

13. Use the remaining fabric to make a left and right front wing. Cut out all the pieces with pinking shears. Repeat with the remaining colours, cutting away each section of the template as you go.
≫⟶

15. When you have all the pieces, compile the wings in the correct order making sure you line up the top straight edges. Pin together through all layers. Sew along the top edge of each section.

sew

17. Place the right and left wings right side together on top of the back wing, matching the top edges, and pin. Sew together through all layers.

sew

16. Take the right and left wing and place in position on the front of your poncho. Where the wings meet the neckline, fold the wing inwards so it follows the line of the neck, crease and pin through the wing layers only.

To attach to the poncho

18. Open it out flat and place the wings on top, lining up the seam with the poncho's shoulder crease. Pin then sew in place.

↦ Alternatively make the basic poncho shape then use fabric paints to paint the wings.

sew

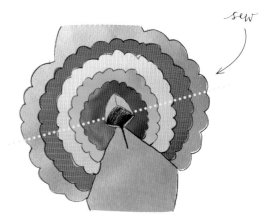

SCALLOP CAPE

To make this more delicate version of the poncho, simply follow steps 11-15 on the previous pages. Use a variety of patterned lightweight fabrics like chiffons, thin cottons and sequined gauzes.

Make two fabric pompoms (see page 66 for instuctions) and attach to the front of the cape. Use these or a small decorative clasp to hold the cape together.

Plaited basket

A basket is perfect for carrying round the festival site, easy to throw things into and more spacious than you think. There is a lot of plaiting involved in this one but treat it as a mindful medative exercise and it'll soon be done.

you will need

1.5 m lightweight calico ✻ Safety pins ✻ Basic sewing kit ✻ 50 cm hessian
Rectangular washing up bowl ✻ 1 litre of paint ✻ Two thin bamboo canes

To plait the material

- Rip the calico into 5 cm wide strips. If it's hard to rip, start each length with a little snip from a pair of scissors.

- Take three strips, lay them one on top of another and fasten together with a safety pin. Plait. When you approach the end of the strips add more by wrapping the existing strips around the new ones and continue until you have made a 7 m plait. Fasten the end with a safety pin.

To shape the basket

- Take one end of the plait, remove the pin and begin spiralling the plait around itself. Sew the coils of the plait together as you go with an overstitch.

- The plait will start to make an oval shape as you continue spiralling it around. On roughly the sixth spiral begin shaping the basket by turning the plait back on itself when it is at one of the short sides of the oval (**A**).

- Turn again when it reaches the other side (**B**) so that the plait will continue the way it was originally going.

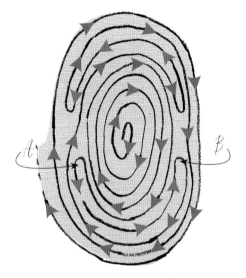

- You may find you have a big gap between the coils where you have turned the plait; when you sew these coils together pull the thread tight and the plait will start to curve upwards, forming a basket shape.

- Repeat the coiling and turning process at the other end of the oval then continue coiling the plait right around the basket for another five coils or until the plait runs out. Fix the ends of the plait firmly in place with several over stitches so it doesn't unravel. ⯈⯈→

to make the handle

⅔ Take the hessian and cut into 5 cm wide strips. Plait this together as before until you have approximately 2 m in length. Sew one coil around the top of the basket, cut when finished, then sew firmly in place as before.

⅔ Cut the remaining plait into two 45 cm long pieces. Sew one end of each together on each side of your basket. Make sure they are securely sewn in place.

to dip the basket

⅔ Dipping the basket bottom in paint makes it nice and strong and helps it keep its shape, while also providing a solid bottom that will protect the contents from damp grass.

⅔ Fill the washing up bowl with 5 cm of paint (this will seem like a lot of paint, but you can pour it back into the tin when you have finished the project and use it again). Dip the basket into the paint, pressing down on the base inside to get the bottom right in. The paint will rise up and cover the base and start creeping up the sides.

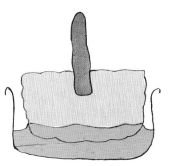
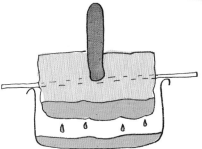

⅔ When you are happy with the paint coverage lift the basket out and suspend it above the bowl by pushing the two bamboo canes through the sides of the basket, then sitting them on the edge of the bowl. This allows the paint to drip back into the bowl as the basket dries. Alternatively you could hang the basket from a line above the bowl or some old cardboard– anything to catch the drips.

⅔ Leave the basket to dry completely before you use it.

⟶ If you don't have enough paint to dip the basket, in, simply use a medium size paintbrush and paint the base and sides of the basket, then leave to dry upside down. A couple of coats of paint should do the trick and work just as well.

Make-up

Festivals are the ideal place to break away from your everyday mascara and eyeliner routine. It's time to crack out the face paints and glitter.,

When space in your rucksack is tight, you don't want to be taking a bulging make-up bag with you. A few pots of kids' face paint and a selection of make-up pencils means you will have all the tools you need to create some extra special looks. Aim to take a selection of bright colours for lips and eyes, a fine make-up brush (a 6 mm concealer brush is perfect), mascara and of course glitter, stick on gems and sequins are also a must.

LEOPARD PRINT EYES

1. Sweep a pale shimmer eyeshadow over your eyelid and blend out into the socket. Line your upper lash line. Use a brown liner then gold liquid liner on top for a stronger look.

2. Use a brown eye pencil or liner to draw rough horseshoe shapes on the lid and around your eyes. Add small dots between the horseshoes. For a bolder look use electric blue.

3. Fill inside the horseshoes with a different coloured pencil; gold is subtle or try hot pink or a liquid glitter eyeliner to really stand out. Finish with mascara and a dusting of glitter.

FESTIVAL FLOWERS

1. The strong colours of kids' facepaints are perfect for these flowers. Use the rounded end of a make-up brush to form the petals. Wet the facepaint slightly then dab the end in and press onto the skin.

2. Start the largest flower diagonally above the end of your eyebrow. Five circles make the petals. Place a stick-on gem in the centre . Repeat with smaller flowers down your cheek and over your brow.

3. Join the flowers with a trail of small dots in lime green, white and gold. Place a gem in the inner corner of your eye. If you don't have adhesive gems use a small blob of eyelash glue or vaseline. Dust with glitter.

103

Friendship bracelets

Make loads of these simple bracelets to win yourself lots of new friends at festival time. Trade them for dry socks and cider.

FISHTAIL BRACELET

This bracelet is a very stylish version of a traditional
plait using eight strands instead of three.

1. Cut four strands of embroidery
thread 1 m long. Fold in half and
knot with a loop. Fix to a solid
surface, by hooking round a nail in
a bench or pinning to your
trousers. Separate the threads so
you have one of each colour on
each side.

2. Take the outside colour strand
from the right and bring to the
centre. Repeat with the left
and place under the right hand
strand. Pull tight by gathering up
all the strands in two hands and
pull outwards slightly.

3. Take the next two strands and
repeat the previous step.

4. Keep going until you have made
a long enough braid to wrap
around your wrist once or twice.
Finish off by threading the strands
onto a button or bead that fits
snugly through the loop and knot.

→ This braid works great with
thicker twines, wools and makes
a beautiful alternative to the
normal hair plait. ≫→

MINI BELL BRACELET

Never get lost in the crowd with the pretty bell bracelet.
If you can't find tiny bells small beads also look cute.

1, Cut two strands of embroidery thread 1 m long. Fold in half and knot with a loop. Cut away one of the strands close to the knot so you are left with three strands. Fix to a solid surface by hooking round a nail in a bench or pinning to your trousers. Then begin plaiting the strands.

2, Plait about 4 cm then slide a small bell or bead onto both the outer strands. Continue plaiting for a couple of turns then add two more bells.

3, Repeat step 2 until you have made about 10 cm of your bell bracelet.

4, Continue plaiting for another 4 cm then thread the strands through a pretty button and tie tightly on the reverse. Use the starting loop as a button hole to fasten.

KNOTTED STRIPE BRACELET

This braid is more often seen decorating dreadlocks and festival hair. It's also a really quick way of making a bracelet.

1. Cut four strands of embroidery thread 60 cm long. Fold in half and knot with a loop. Fix to a solid surface by hooking round a nail in a bench or pinning to your trousers. Lay the strands out straight and separate one off to the left hand side.

2. Take this strand over the others to the right.

3. Wrap this strand around the back of the others and up through the loop (essentially tying a knot). Pull tightly upwards towards the large knot.

4. Repeat steps 2 and 3 with this thread till you get bored then choose another and start building up a pattern. Continue until the bracelet is approximately 10 cm long. To finish tie all strands in a big knot.

DECORATED
TROLLEYS

Some festivals have trolleys that you can hire when you arrive, to help you lug all your camping equipment from your car to the campsite. These trolleys are brilliant and often used for the rest of the festival to pull sleeping babies and toddlers around in when it all gets too much! They are also a good place to stash your bags, booze and biscuits. Wheelbarrows, porters wheels, wheeled shopping bags (anything with the word wheel in the title basically) is handy on site unless it rains and then you may need a tow truck to get you out of the mud.

If you hire a trolley at the festival take battery or solar powered fairy lights and cheap bunches of fake flowers to personalise it and make it easy to identify. Bunting, streamers and balloons all add to the festival feel.

If you have your own trolley you can take more time over the personalisation. Paint an old metal cage trolley with a white primer, then spray paint with gold paint, to add some glitz. Then line three sides with some old hessian so little bits and pieces don't fall through the holes. Decorate the final side with fabric flowers woven through the cage and wrap the handle with rope.

Bamboo cane streamers

These bamboo streamers are a great way of livening up your campsite. The pretty streamers flutter in the breeze and the colourful canes are perfect for marking out your territory.

you will need

8 bamboo canes, 1 m tall

Spray paint in various colours

Twine, wool or string in various colours

Washi tapes in various patterns

Fluro gaffer tape

Mallet and chisel

Several lightweight fabrics 10 cm wide and 1 m in length (nylon, silk, polyester)

Lay several canes side by side on a flat surface - an old sheet or piece of cardboard - ideally outside. Spray paint strips of colour across the canes, varying the width of the stripes to build up a pattern. Roll the canes over and continue until all the sides are covered. Allow to dry.

Wrap twine or wool around the canes where two paint colours join, holding the ends of the twine in place with a length of washi or gaffer tape. Repeat along the cane.

Use a mallet and chisel to split the end of one cane about 10 cm down. Holding the cane in an upright position, put the wider end of the cane against a wall. Place the chisel on the top of the cane in the middle. Tap gently with the mallet to embed the chisel then whack to split.

Take three or four strips of fabric, place them one on top of the other and slide down into the split of the cane, where they should wedge in nicely. Now sit back and wait for a breeze!

Giant bunny bow

**If a big crazy headdress isn't for you this gold lace headpiece
is a more sophisticated take on traditional bunny ears.
These require no sewing and are easy to make.**

you will need

25 x 60 cm lace fabric ✶ All-purpose glue ✶ Old paintbrush ✶ Basic sewing kit ✶ Gold headband

Cut the lace fabric in half lengthways so you have two 12.5 cm wide rectangles. Place one on top of the other, wrong sides together, and lay flat on a surface protected by a plastic sheeting or a bin bag (to stop the glue sticking to the table top).

Mix 50 ml of glue with a couple of tablespoons of water then paint this mixture onto the lace. Use the paintbrush to work the glue into all the nooks and crannies of the lace. When you have completely covered one side turn the lace over and do the back. Leave to dry overnight.

When the lace is dry it should be much stiffer. If it still seems floppy, paint on some more glue then leave to dry again.

Enlarge the ear template from page 138 cut out and pin to the lace. Cut out the ears.

Tie the ears in a knot around the headband; this may be a little tricky due to the stiffness of the lace, but it will work. Pull into shape when done. A couple of stitches between the lace and the headband will hold the ears securely in place.

Give the ears another coat of glue on both sides to stiffen even further. Leave to dry overnight.

These ears work brilliantly with other kinds of thin fabrics - try patterned cottons or linens. Also try spray painting the tips in a contrasting colour or coat in glitter for extra sparkle.

Silk flower headdress

What could be more festival fabulous that this beautiful, exotic flower headdress. The real flower garlands are ubiquitous at all festivals now, but this project offers something beautiful and a little longer lasting.

you will need

Fine synthetic fabrics like silky satins, tulle, or organza (works better than real silk)
Sharp scissors ✕ A candle ✕ Needle and thread ✕ 50–60 cm coloured elastic for the
headband this can be up to 2 cm wide.

Unlike real flowers these won't wilt and dry out, instead they will stay looking fresh and gorgeous, whether you are staying for a day or a week. You can also take it home with you, and hang it in your room to remind you of wonderful times.

✄ Begin by making one flower first from beginning to end so that you understand the process, then you can prepare lots of strips so that you can work on each step on all of your flowers at the same time.

✄ Start by selecting a collection of fine fabric scraps and remnants in a variety of lengths between 15 and 35 cm with widths of 2 to 4 cm or anywhere in between.

To make the petals
✄ Beginning with a 35 x 4 cm strip, fold over the end of the fabric by approximately 2 cm, then continue folding until you have a bundle that is 2 x 4 cm.

✄ With a pair of sharp scissors cut through all the layers making a petal shape, beginning a quarter of the way up. Open out and you will have a series of petals all joined together.

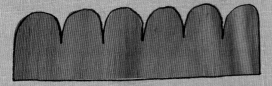

✄ Once you have made a few flowers you may want to start experimenting by cutting narrower, taller petals like chrysanthemum or shorter stubby petals like poppies. ≫→

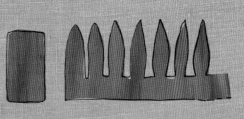

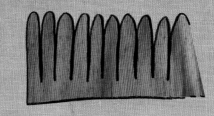

The process is surprisingly simple, but not quick as it may take one or two experiments before you get it right. It is worth pursuing as it really is easy once you know how.

To age the edges

Light a candle and CAREFULLY singe the edges of each petal by passing it through the tip of the candle. The synthetic fabric will become hard and slightly curled. Touch the flame with the fabric just enough so that the heat of the candle melts the edges. It doesn't have to be perfect, but it does take a bit of time to get right. Leave to cool. The result is worth the effort and you will find that the odd mistake where a petal distorts can look quite authentic in the final result.

If you do decide to use pure silk be EXTRA careful as the fabric can quickly disappear completely and also burn your fingers in the process. However with practice it can look beautiful, like the gentle browning of rose petals at the end of the season.

To make the flowers

When all the edges are singed, thread a needle and begin rolling the length of petals around on itself, sewing through the bottom edge joining all the layers together as you wrap. Don't roll it too tight or too loose, as it will naturally form a flower shape and you will be able to tell when it looks right.

sew

Once it is completely rolled, make sure it is securely stitched together by passing the needle through all the layers, from one side to the other a few times, then fold down some of the petals. Manipulate by hand to get the desired effect.

To make the headdress

Make a selection of flowers in lots of different colours, shapes and sizes before you construct your headdress, in the same way as you would make a bouquet. When you have more than enough, lay them out in a line taking into consideration which combination of colours looks best. Fill in any gaps with smaller flowers here and there.

Cut a piece of elastic about 50 cm long or whatever feels comfortable around your crown, not too tight or too loose, and stitch it together to make a band.

Sew each flower onto the band using an overstitch, by wrapping the sewing thread around the whole elastic, NOT through it and then through the flower. This method allows you to move the flowers along the band, bunching them closer together or further apart. Once all the flowers attached, the headdress is ready wear.

Also you can attach single flowers to hair clips by sewing through the flower and overstitching it on one side of a kirby grip. These can be worn in a row as shown here or singly if you prefer.

You can also attach a few to a ribbon and wear as a choker around your neck or stitch to a safety pin and wear as a corsage.

Showertime dress

A stylish dress made from towelling is the perfect multi-functional garment to slip on when you head to the festival showers. Don't forget your flip flops though!

you will need

Two white flannels ✳ Basic sewing kit ✳ Two 60 x 90 cm rectangles of blue towelling material or bath towel of similar measurements ✳ 1 m piping cord 1 cm diameter ✳ White gaffer tape or similar

Festival showers... they always leave a lot to be desired – long queues (good for making friends), questionable hot water and skanky cubicle floors. If you do feel the need to brave the showers during your festival stay, this dress will make you the best dressed person in the queue. Simply slip over your head when you've finished showering and you can spend as little time as possible drying off. The big pockets come in handy for toiletries and clean pants.

To make the pockets

✄ Cut out two rectangle 18 cm wide by 20 cm deep from the flannels. If your flannels have fancy edges use these for the top of your pockets.

✄ Use a zigzag switch on all the raw edges to prevent fraying and then turn over a 0.5 cm hem and press.

✄ Pin the pockets to one of the blue rectangles 8 cm from the bottom edge and 7 cm from the sides. Machine sew in place.

To shape the armholes

✄ Place the two rectangles on top of each other, right sides together. Find the centre of the top short side and mark. Measure 20 cm each way from this point and mark with a pin, then measure 35 cm down from the top on each edge and mark. Draw diagonal lines between these points to create the armhole shape. Cut away the excess fabric on both rectangles.

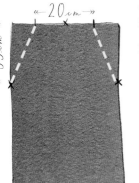

✄ Leaving a 0.5 cm seam allowance sew up both of the long sides of the rectangles, until you reach the bottom of the armholes. Use a zigzag stitch on the raw edges first to prevent fraying.

✄ Zigzag stitch the four raw edges of the armholes. Turn over a 0.5 cm hem on each side, press and sew.

✄ At the bottom of the dress turn over a 1 cm double hem, press and sew all around.

To make the cord channel

✄ On the front of the dress turn and press a 1 cm hem then turn again by a further 5 cm, press then sew. Repeat with the back rectangle.

✄ To stop the cord fraying, tape the ends with gaffer tape.

✄ Starting at the front right hand side of the dress feed the cord through the neck channels. Tie with a reef knot.

↝ This simple dress looks gorgeous made in lightweight cottons or silks with a ribbon at the neck. You can also amend the pattern by adding an extra 60 cm (depending on height) to the length to make an elegant maxi dress. Leave the bottom 70 cm of one side seam unsewn to avoid a hobbled walk.

Patchwork tent

If you can't get to a festival this year, this tent will add a little festival vibe to any back garden. On site this tent works well as a shade from the midday sun or an emergency spare room

you will need

2.5 x 1.4-m wide fabric ✶ Two 45 x 60 cm fabric rectangles ✶ Basic sewing kit ✶ 50 x 4-cm wide elastic
Tailors' chalk ✶ *For the window* 50 x 40 cm netting ✶ 1.2 m x 2-cm wide ribbon ✶ One single sheet (optional)
Find branches on site or cut dowel the right lengths before you go. Five 140 cm long branches
One 160 cm long branch for the cross beam ✶ Thin rope for lashing

If you are making the main body of the tent in a patchwork style, sew all the pieces together until you have a rectangle measuring 2.5 x 1.4 m. Turn a 2 cm hem on all the edges and sew.

Cut the elastic into four equal lengths. Fold each in half and pin one to each corner, on the long edges.

To make the window.

Flip the tent so you have the wrong side facing you. Measure 40 cm in and 60 cm up from one corner of the rectangle. This point will be the bottom right hand corner of the window. From this point measure and draw a 45 x 40 cm rectangle. Cut away the fabric inside this rectangle until you are 1cm from the drawn line.

At each corner cut a diagonal snip towards the drawn line, then fold and press a 1 cm hem. Take the netting rectangle and pin in place over the window hole and sew.

To make the blind.

Pin the two 45 x 60 cm rectangles together right sides facing then sew with a 5 mm seam allowance. Leave a turning gap of 10 cm in one of the long edges.

Turn right side out and press flat (make sure you press the raw edges from the turning hole inwards).

Cut the 1.2 m of ribbon in half then fold each piece so you roughly have 40 cm and 20 cm sections.

Place the ribbons over the blind on the long side with the turning hole, about 10 cm in from each end. Make sure the longer pieces are at the back of the blind. Pin in place.

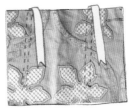

Place the blind on top of the tent over the window and pin in place. Machine sew the blind onto the tent along the top edge, over the ribbons and the turning hole.

If you wish to line your tent

Make another tent as per the instructions above using the sheet but without the blind. You can either sew these two tents together or simply put them one on top of the other when erecting the tent. This is useful if you wish to remove the outer tent if it gets especially hot.

To erect the tent

This is easier to do with two people. Take two of the shorter poles, overlap them leaving about 20 cm at the top and lash together using a thin rope. Repeat with the other two poles.

Place the cross pole in the crux of one of the lashed pairs and lash all three together. Repeat with the second pair at the other end.

Hang the tent over the cross pole and stretch the elastic over each foot of the four legs. Adjust the angle of the legs to make sure the tent is stable. For added stability lash the fifth pole into the rear pair to form a tripod.

119

Pompom necklace

This is such a fun and colourful necklace. The more colours and trimmings the better! Use the tassels and pompoms to make matching earrings.

you will need

Pink, purple and turquoise wool ✻ Basic sewing kit ✻ Pink, yellow and beige twine Gold, blue, yellow and turquoise embroidery thread ✻ 35 cm small pompom trim

❧ Make one turquoise, two purple and two pink 4 cm diameter pompoms (see page 67 for instructions).

To make the tassels

1. Wind the thread around your index, middle and ring fingers about 60 times or until you have approximately 1 cm thickness of thread. Slip this from your fingers and thread another piece of cotton, around 15 cm long, through one end of the loop and tie tightly to hold all the strands together.

2. Tie another strand of cotton around all the strands about 1 cm from the top. Cut through the bottom loops to make the tassel. Make two gold and two yellow tassels.

To make the necklace.

❧ Cut four strands of the twine each 2 m long. Fold in half so you have eight strands. Plait into a fishtail plait following the instructions on page 105. Plait until it is about 70 cm long or to suit.

❧ Find the midpoint of the plait and mark with a pin. Take the pompom trim and place the mid point of this on to the mid point of the plait. Pin together.

❧ Sew the trim to the plait using cross stitch. Finish off the ends by binding the trim to the plait and wrapping the coloured cottons around both the trim and the plait. Secure the ends of the cottons by sewing them into the plait a couple of times. Repeat this process at intervals down the length of the necklace for further decoration.

❧ Cut away every other pompom from the trim to make space for the larger pompoms and tassels you have made.

❧ Fix the pompoms and tassels to the necklace by sewing them on securely.

GLASS HOLDER

you will need

Coloured twine or string, *we used Nutscene coloured twine but you could use any household or garden twine.* ⚬ Crochet hook size 4.5 mm (US size 7)

- Make 6ch and join with a sl st in a loop.

- Round 1: 1 ch (counts as first dc), 1dc into st at the base of 1-ch, then 2dc into each st to end of round. *(12 sts)*

- Round 2: 3 ch (counts as first tr), 1tr into st at the base of 3-ch, then 2tr into each st to end of round. *(24 sts)*

- Round 3: work 2tr into the base of the turning chain, *miss two spaces then work 3tr into third space, repeat from * six times more, join to second of turning chain with a sl st. Make 3 turning chain.

- Round 4-6: Work 2tr into the base of the turning chain, then *work 3tr into each space between the 3tr clusters from Round 3, repeat from * six times more, join to second of turning chain with to second of turning chain with a sl st. Make 2 turning chain.

- Round 7: work 1dc into base of the turning chain, then work 1dc into the top of each treble all around (24sts), join with sl st to turning chain. Fastern off.

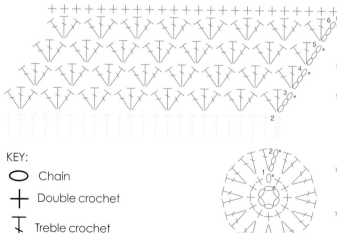

➤ If working from the chart remember that this pattern is worked clockwise in the round and NOT from right to left.

⟶ See page 123 for instructions on strap.

⟶ Due to the stretch of this crochet stitch, these holders can accommodate glasses with a diameter of between 8 cm and 12cm.

⟶ For shorter glasses skip row 6 and for shorter strap make less chain.

⟶ For striped glass holders similar to the bottle holder, change the colour of string on each round.

KEY:
- ⬭ Chain
- ✛ Double crochet
- ⊤ Treble crochet

Abbreviations

sl st Slip stitch

ch chain

dc double crochet

tr treble

turning chain is counted as 1 stitch.

Feather garland

These fabric feathers look great draped around your tent, but they also make a wonderful necklace or headdress. Use brightly coloured sparkly fabrics for added spangle.

you will need

2.5 m garden twine ✶ Piece plastic ✶ All-purpose glue
Old paintbrush ✶ Various patterned cotton fabrics, approx A4 size
Pompoms ✶ Large darning needle ✶ Scissors
✶ Wooden and silver beads with large holes to decorate

These feathers are so versatile. They make a lovely tent decoration strung on a garland as seen here. Bunch them all up together and add to a plaited length of twine for a bold necklace, or add several to a headdress, or use them as finishing touches for the Festival Mandala on page 64.

- Cut the fabrics into various sized rectangles, the smallest ones need to be 11 x 4 cm and the largest 22 x 7 cm. Make sure you have two rectangles of each size so if you are making a garland of 30 feathers. You will need 60 varying size rectangles.

- Partner up the rectangles so you have different fabrics in each pair. For some of the feathers you could join and create different pieces of fabric to make up the rectangles a patchwork effect. Anything goes with these!

- Lay all the paired up rectangles on a flat surface covered with plastic (a bin bag will do). Mix approximately 50 mls of all-purpose glue with two tablespoons of water and then paint this mixture onto all the rectangles. When done flip them over and paint the reverse. Leave to dry overnight.

- When dry take one of the rectangles and cut a feather shape from it (you can use the templates on page 139 as guides or just freestyle your own).

- Fold the feather lengthways down the middle from top to bottom.

- Down the raw edges of the feather cut little angled snips making sure you stop about 0.5 cm from the middle fold. Vary the positions of the snips on each feather, some can have several and some only a few.

- Shape the feather further by pinching along the spine and pulling into a curve.

- When you have made all the feathers, start threading them onto the twine using a large darning needle. Push the needle through the quill of each feather.

- As you thread the feathers on, alternate with the pompoms and beads.

- For added sparkle coat the tips of the feathers in all-purpose glue then sprinkle with fine glitter.

127

Jam jar chandelier

Sparkly lights are the perfect festival decor but the lack of electricity limits most festival goers to battery operated fairy lights, torches or candles. Simply add luxury with this easy-to-make Jam Jar Chandelier and impress your fellow campers!

you will need

Metal herb dryer ✶ Pliers ✶ 5 mm thickness garden wire ✶ Chalk based paint ✶ Paintbrush
A selection of different sized glass jars, 4 jam jars and 6 shallow glass ramekin style jars
Chicken wire enough to wrap around 4 jam jars ✶ Florists' wire or fine galvanised wire ✶ 10 tea lights

Made from a metal herb dryer, ten jam jars, chicken wire and tea lights this project is not only practical, but looks gorgeous and will add a little sparkle to your camping area!

You will need a herb dryer for this project. These readily available and easy to buy online. (Check the suppliers on page 141).

Originally all nine of the hooks will be hanging from the central ring of your herb dryer. To create the layered effect for your chandelier use pliers to remove three of the V-shaped hooks then reattach them so that they hang alternately between the six remaining 'V''s from the first layer.

To make a new hook use 5 mm garden wire and attach it to the middle of the chandelier, at the top, just below the hanging hook.

Paint the chandelier with a chalk based paint.

To make the lanterns
Wrap a piece of pre-cut chicken wire around a jam jar, twisting the ends together with pliers to form a vertical seam and moulding the bottom edge under the base of the jar to hold it in place.

Weave a piece of thin galvanised wire, fuse wire would also work just as well, through the top edge of the chicken wire, drawing it in towards the neck of the jar. Make a handle by cutting a length of wire, long enough to stretch around the neck of the jar and to make a double twisted handle.

Wrap the wire around the neck of the jar then twist the two ends together using pliers, until it is tight and secure around the neck. Continue winding the two ends together creating a barley twist effect.

Fold over to make a handle, threading one of the ends under the wire ring around the neck of the jar, then join it to the remaining end and twist it together again to hold in place. Snip off to create a neat finish, then continue to make the hanging handles for the remaining six small jars in the same way.

Hang the chandelier from a branch then place the tea lights in each jar and light them with a taper.

Campsite lantern

By day your container is an essential provider of thirst quenching water and by night an atmospheric lantern to light up your tent. Create a magical scene when you shine a torch through a container of water, the light is magnified - is much brighter and goes further than the light from the torch alone. Clever stuff.

you will need

Tracing paper ✗ Pencil ✗ White sticky back plastic ✗ Opaque sticky back plastic
Scissors or craft knife and cutting mat ✗ Large water container ✗ Headtorch
For the disco light Small clear water bottles ✗ Glow sticks

🌿 Trace the different elements of the illustration above onto the reverse of the sticky back plastic. Trace the orange coloured sections onto the opaque and the grey coloured onto the white. Cut these out carefully using a craft knife and cutting mat or small scissors.

🌿 Before peeling the protective backing from the sticky back plastic, plan your design on the container. The shape of your bottle will determine the final design. When you are happy with it get sticking.

🌿 Light the lantern by fixing the headtorch around the bottle so the torch part is at the back of the bottle. Turn on when it gets too dark to find your pyjamas.

To make the disco lights
🌿 Fill smaller bottles with water and remove any labels. Crack the glow sticks to activate them and drop in one stick per bottle. Replace cap.

⟿ Probably best not to drink the water from these bottles even if you're desperate.

Fold out picnic hamper

This is no ordinary picnic hamper ... it's also a picnic blanket with a waterproof bottom. Find the perfect spot, sit down unpop the sides of the bag and you're good to lay the table!

you will need

Basic sewing kit ✳ Cardboard ✳ Pencil ✳ 1.5 m oil cloth ✳ Scissors
Various pieces of fabric to make a patchwork cross approx 1 x 1.6 m ✳ 1.5 m large popper tape

❧ First make a template from grey cardboard. This will dictate the size of your picnic hamper's base. A 34 x 25 cm landscape rectangle is a good size. Draw a vertical line down the middle of this rectangle.

❧ Lay several sheets of newspaper on the floor and tape together. This will become your pattern.

❧ Lay the card template in the middle of the paper and draw around. Then using the tempate draw two rectangles, one above and one below the first. These are the long sides.

❧ For the short sides and flaps you need a measurement that is one and a half rectangles long on each side. Place the template on the pattern so the short edge butts up with the left hand short edge of the first rectangle drawn. Draw one half rectangle and one full one. Repeat on the right hand side side.

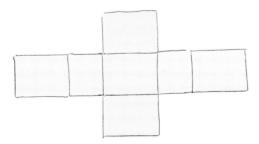

❧ On the pattern draw quarter circles joining up the sides of the hamper. Cut out the pattern. If you have used several pieces of paper make sure they are taped together securely.

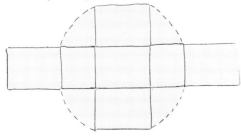

❧ Lay the pattern onto the reverse of the oilcloth, draw around and cut out, leaving a 1 cm seam allowance all around. Cut out the shape.

to make the bag lining

❧ If your lining is made from one piece of material cut out the pattern as you did for the oilcloth above.

❧ If you are making a lining like we have here then begin building up a patchwork pattern using your fabrics. Try and make the patchwork in blocks the same size as the original rectangle of the bag as this helps the bag fold up neatly. You can make the rectangles up using smaller shapes but keep to the three main strips. Remember to leave a 1 cm seam allowance around each of your patchwork pieces.

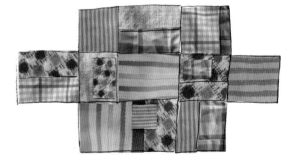

❧ When you are happy with the layout of the patchwork sew the pieces together. Start by sewing the smaller pieces to form rectangles, then sew these together to form strips and finally sew the three strips together.

❧ Place the pattern onto the reverse of the patchwork. Draw round leaving a 1 cm seam allowance then cut out.

To make the pockets

❧ Pockets are useful for picnic cutlery and other small bits. For a cutlery pocket cut a rectangle of fabric 21 x 13 cm. Turn and press a 1cm double hem on one long side, then sew. ≫→

On the three remaining sides turn and press a 0.5 cm hem. Pin the pocket in place on the patchwork (on one of the side walls) then sew around the three sides. Make cutlery dividers by sewing two straight lines of stitches down the pocket. Make other pockets to suit.

To add the poppers

Take the oilcloth and on the reverse draw out the rectangle pattern. This makes it easier to position the poppers.

On each of the quarter circles, measure 2 cm in from the short edge of tthe long side and 2 cm up from the short side edges. Cut a strip of 4 poppers (possibly more depending on the size of your poppers) separate the poppers and pin the halves at right angles to each other at the points marked.

Repeat with the other three corners. Sew in place. Using a zigzag stitch to cover the raw edges of the popper tape.

Place the oilcloth and liner together right sides facing. Pin then sew together, leaving a 15 cm turning hole along one long straight edges. Notch the fabric around the curves of the bag then turn right side out and carefully press. Hand sew up the turning hole.

To make the carry straps

Cut two strips of oil cloth 8 cm x 1m long (join up several pieces if necessary. Patchwork together 2 strips the same measurements from the remaining fabric. Pin one oilcloth and one fabric strip right sides together then machine sew along both long sides with a 0.5 cm seam allowance. Turn right side out, making sure to tuck the raw edges of the open ends inwards, then press (be careful not to melt the oilcloth). Repeat with the second strap.

Place the unfolded bag on a flat surface oilcloth side uppermost. Place one end of one strap in the centre of the base 5 cm in from one side. Pin in place. Fold the handle around at the top and bring it back down onto the bag in the same position on the other side of the rectangle. Pin in place then repeat with the other handle.

Sew the handles to the bag by running a line of stitches up the sides, top and bottom.

To constuct the bag

To fold the bag up simply popper each corresponding side together, folding the quarter circles of excess fabric inwards into the bag. Fold the flaps over the bag. You can add a button and loop to keep it securely closed if you wish.

FESTIVAL CALENDAR

MAR/APR/MAY

THIS IS NOT A LOVE SONG France Indie music festival in Nimes at the beginning of the French festival season. *thisisnotalovesong.fr*

SXSW USA SXSW Film and SXSW Interactive both now combine with SXSW music creating the perfect creative festival. *sxsw.co.uk*

COACHELLA USA Coachella sells out even before the lineup is announced. Dress to impress. *coachella.com*

MAWAZINE Morrocco 9 days of eclectic and diverse music can be heard over six stages in Rabat. *festivalmawazine.ma*

JUNE

GLASTONBURY UK 'Entering Glastonbury is like entering another world'. The Godfather of all festivals. *glastonburyfestivals. co.uk*

ROCK WERCHTER Belgium Established in the 1970's this rock festival is now one of the biggest in Europe. *rockwerchter.be*

PINKPOP Netherlands According to the *Guinness Book of Records*, Pinkpop is the oldest annual festival in the world. *pinkpop.nl*

BONNAROO USA Escape into 700 acres of Fresh Tennessee air green grass & trees to find excitement and entertainment. *bonnaroo.com*

HURRICANE Germany Located in Scheessel Hurricane is the sister festival to Southside in Neuhausen ob Eckso *hurricane. southside.de*

PRIMAVERA SOUND Spain A festival for true music aficionados. *primaverasound.es*

SONAR Spain Sónar in Barcelona is the festival for electronica. Sonar also organises festivals every year in other cities. *sonar.es*

GOVERNORS BALL USA Held on Randall's Island in New York City features an array of music styles. *governorsballmusicfestival.com*

ISLE OF WIGHT UK This is one of the original Summer of Love festivals. With over 600,000 people attending in 1970 to watch the likes of Jimi Hendrix, The Doors and The Who. Revived in 2002. *isleofwightfestival.com*

JULY

ATP Iceland According to Nick Cave ATP is "My favourite festival, in my favourite country" nothing more to say. *atpfestival.com*

CAMP BESTIVAL UK Kid friendly sister festival to Bestival. Great music and entertainment for festival goers of all ages. *campbestival.net*

FUJI ROCK FESTIVAL Japan A magical event in Naeba. A stunning mountain setting and a friendly crowd. *fujirock-eng.com*

ROSKILDE Denmark A not for profit festival that supports the development of music culture and humanism. *roskilde-festival.dk*

EXIT Serbia This festival in Novi Sad began in 2000 in a University park fighting for freedom in Serbia and the Balkans. *exitfest.org*

BENICASSIM Spain This four-day music festival is full of sun, sand and amazing music, what more could you want? *benicassimfestival.co.uk*

TOMORROW'S LAND Belgium The largest annual electronic music festival in the world, it takes place outside Antwerp and has sister festivals in Brazil (May) & the USA (August). *tomorrowland.com*

LATITUDE UK Known for its elements of theatre, art, comedy, cabaret, poetry, politics, dance and literature as well as great music acts. Set in the Suffolk countryside. *latitudefestival.com*

SPLENDOUR IN THE GRASS Australia One of the best and largest Winter music festivals in OZ. *splendourinthegrass.com*

POHODA Slovakia Meaning relax, an eclectic mix of rock, dance, hip hop and chamber music. *pohodafestival.sk*

DOUR Belgium Began 25 years ago with an audience of 2000 it now attractes over 150,000. *dourfestival.eu*

LATITUDE   NO.6 FESTIVAL   ROSKILDE   BESTIVAL

SOMERSAULT FESTIVAL UK A summer camp of great indie music, adventure & outdoor living in the heart of South West of England. *somersaultfestival.com*

PORT ELIOT UK Port Eliot's hidden corner of Cornwall makes a festival experience like no other. A celebration of words, music, ideas, nature, food, fashion, flowers, laughter, exploration and fun. Truly magical. If you only ever go to one festival make it this one. *porteliotfestival.com*

AUGUST

SHAMBALA UK Enchanted Woodlands, surreal sculptures and creative workshops make this a great wild event for all ages. *shambalafestival.org*

WILDERNESS UK A contender for the UK's coolest festival. A beautiful setting for beautiful people. *wildernessfestival.com*

SECRET GARDEN PARTY UK The original boutique festival set in the grounds of a Georgian farm house in deepest Cambridgeshire. *secretgardenparty.com*

OYA Norway This uber hip festival attracts a top lineup. *oyafestivalen.com*

FLOW Finland Helsinki hosts this super cool festival that attracts all the usual top indie bands to its environmentally aware urban location. *flowfestival.com*

WAY OUT WEST Sweden Not a camping festival this is one for the fashionable and those that prefer a shower at the end of each day. *wayoutwest.se*

LOLLAPALOOZA USA This three-day music festival in Chicago has more than 100 alternative rock, punk, heavy metal, comedy and craft booths. *lollapalooza.com*

OSHEAGA Canada With a huge and impressive line up this Montreal festival is the big one for Canada. *osheaga.com*

SZIGET Hungary Sziget takes place on an island in the Danube. *szigetfestival.com*

OFF Poland This medium sized festival is set in luscious countryside but close to the city. Alternative music and left field performers. *off-festival.pl*

THE GREEN MAN FESTIVAL UK Set among the Black Mountains this is the go to festival if you are looking for a refreshingly independent family run festival. *greenman.net*

SEPTEMBER

END OF THE ROAD UK Always an impeccable music lineup here and a must for musos, A magical garden setting with comedy, hula-hooping and a literary stage run by Julian Marsh. *endoftheroadfestival.com*

BURNING MAN USA This legendary event in the Nevada desert mixes Pagan traditions with tribal culture to create a primordial party. *burningman.org*

ELECTRIC PICNIC Ireland Set amid rolling lawns on a beautiful 600 acre estate outside Dublin be prepared to find Irish magic amid the music, art, theatre, and gourmet food. *electricpicnic.ie*

FESTIVALNO6 UK A festival unlike any other, in the amazing intimate venue of Port Merion, Wales. Arts and Culture are an integral part of what makes this an utterly unique festival. *festivalnumber6.com*

BESTIVAL UK Another Isle of Wight stalwart, big in style and bigger in fancy dress and dance music this is the UK's end of the festival. season hurrah. *bestival.net*

OCT/NOV

AIRWAVES Iceland Reykjavík is the perfect festival city. Small enough to be welcoming, sophisticated enough to offer culture, great bands, cool clubs, and after-parties all a bus ride away from geysers, waterfalls and lava fields. *icelandairwaves.is*

LE GUESS WHO? Netherlands This festival is held at fifteen different venues, ranging from churches to pop-up stages all in and around Utrecht. *leguesswho.nl*

FALLS FESTIVAL Australia Held across two venues, Marion Bay and Byron Bay, one of Australia's leading festivals *fallsfestival.com*.

DEC/JAN

TRANSMUSICALES France Renowned for revealing the "next big thing" this 4 day event attracts over 60,000 to Rennes, Brittany. *lestrans.com*

CROSSING BORDER Netherlands This festival of literature, music, film and the visual arts is where writers, poets, musicians, filmmakers and artists reign. *crossingborder.nl*

LANEWAY Australia Group of indie music events started in Melbourne and expanded to five cities as well as to Singapore and Detroit. *lanewayfestival.com*

TOMORROWLAND COACHELLA PORT ELIOT

✦ THANK YOU! ✦

So many people have contributed to the making of Festival Fabulous. Christine and Ros would like to thank them all for their time and effort but they want to especially thank the following for their help.

So… All at Quadrille Publishing, especially Lisa Pendreigh and Harriet Butt and to Jane O'Shea for her kind words of support pre the initial planning meeting. To Jane Turnbull, agent. To Joanna Henderson for her amazing photography, above and beyond the call of duty wielding her camera late into the night at festivals, and to Ben Derbyshire and Sebastian Sharples for their few extra shots and a thank you kiss from Ros to Christine for her photographic contributions too. An extra special thanks to our wonderful models used repeatedly throughout the book May Douglas & Isabel Adomakoh-Young

To Shelley Whitehead and Ruth Burtonshaw and all the staff and groundsmen at Dulwich Prep school for being so accommodating while the (Fake) Fabulous Festival shoots were happening.

Thanks so much to Tim from Dub Dub and Away for the generous loan of HONEY the beautiful VW camper van, she was a star. dubdubandaway.com

Thanks to Liz Cocoran for saving the day by lending her bell tent. So easy to put up and definitely the way to camp and to Karen Boatwright for her stylish handmade sleeping bags.

Thank you to the Family Rickards for coining the phrase 'festival time' and to Oliver for embracing the concept!

To all the festivals that have inspired this book but especially to Lady Catherine St Germans at Port Eliot festival for writing the foreword and for the opportunity to run The Badger's Set workshops where lots of the ideas that have ended up in Festival Fabulous were tested. It's an amazing and inspirational festival so huge thanks to all of the team at Port Eliot: Grace, Robin, Helen, Poppy and everyone else who made us feel so welcome.

Thank you for your help at Port Eliot to Martha Skye Murphy and Ceidra Murphy Badger and to the ethereal Jago Rackham and Lowena Victoria for their invaluable help with the workshops providing an air of calm and grace to the proceedings. To all the Badger's Sett crew, Jess and Martha Kilpatrick, Martha Wilmott-Sitwell, Biba, Isla Wickham, Jasmin Derham and Connie Monroe, thank you.

Thank you too, to all at The End of the Road Festival, to the PR team for the last minute access, to author Julian Mash who runs the EOTR Literary Tent and his beautiful wife Gudron Kloepsch and their son Rowan. To Christine and Ros' EOTR insider festival scouts, Martha, and the art school group George (the girl), Annemarie and Rachel, a very special thank you, especially as their tents were dismantled by security guards, thinking they were imposters….all in the line of duty…and a festival tale for another time.

To the models met around and about at EOTR co-erced into being photographed, you were all charming. Isabel Adomakoh-Young, Freya Holmes, Celia Tempest-Radford, Hana Holland, Kim O'Neil, Martha Allsopp, Pixie Paint London, Martha Skye Murphy, George Stone, Annemarie Wadlow, Rachel Tweedy.

To all the festivals around the world for their brilliant PR shots especially Bestival, Tomorrowland, No 6 Festival, Latitude, Rosklide, Port Eliot.

Thanks to Toni Jones (@Mrs_ToniJones) and Saskia Quirke, Tanita Montgomery, Clare Ferguson and Leanne Bayley for all their personal festival photographs that grace the pages of this book. Extra thanks to TJ and Sas for roadtesting some Festival Fabulous headdresses at Bestival and extra extra thanks to TJ and Erica Davies (modernmummusthave.co.uk) for the expert advice on how to pack stylishly for a festival. Thank you Fiona Fletcher for your top make-up tips (fionamfletcher.com.

Christine and Ros would also like to thank the following for their generous sponsorship supplying materials for both this book and The Badgers' Sett workshops: GF Smith, Wilko, Love knitting, Nutscene, Block, Blooming Felt.

Last but not least Christine and Ros would like to thank their parents and families for their help and advice and send love to them all.

They hope they haven't forgotten anyone but if they have it's not intentional, blame living the Festival Fabulous life!

rosbadger.com sewyeah.co.uk
twitter & instagram @rosbadger @sewyeah

PICTURE CREDITS

Project pictures and Port Eliot incidentals by Joanna Henderson joannahenderson.com. Other photography by Christine Leech, Ben Derbyshire, Toni Jones, Tanita Montgomery, Clare Ferguson, Leanne Bayley apart from: p6 Port Eliot Festival Micheal Bowles, p10 Bestival festival Dan Dennison, Roskilde Festival Helena Lundquist, p11 Festival No.6 Danny North, Latitude Festival Rebecca Naen, Tomorrowland Fille Roelants, p23 Roskilide Festival Vegard S. Kristiansen, p27 Port Eliot Festival Micheal Bowles, p43 Port Eliot Festival Fiona Campbell, p61 Roskilide Fesival Christian Hjorth, Latitude Festival Ade More, Roskilide Fesival Christian Hjorth, p136 Latitude Festival Mark Sethi, No.6 Festival Danny North, Roskilide Fesival Christian Hjorth, Bestival Festival Victor Frankowski, Tomorrowland Festival Rutger Geerling, Coachella Festival Leanne Bayley, Port Eliot Festival.

Index

Leave nothing but footprints,
Take nothing but memories.

FAREWELL